THE ROYAL SHAKESPEARE COMPA

The Royal Shakespeare Company is pr
in the world. It has operated in its pres
from the Shakespeare Memorial Thea
widened its repertoire to embrace wo...

Today the RSC has five home theatres. In Stratford the Royal Shakespeare Theatre stages large-scale productions of Shakespeare's plays; the Swan, a galleried Jacobean playhouse, brings to light the plays of many of his neglected contemporaries alongside classics of world theatre, while The Other Place, the company's studio theatre, houses some of the company's most exciting experimental and contemporary work, as well as providing a regular venue for visiting companies and some of the RSC's education work, including the annual Prince of Wales Shakespeare School.

In 1982 the company moved its London home to the Barbican Centre, where in the large-scale Barbican Theatre and the studio-sized Pit Theatre, the company stages new productions as well as the repertoire transferring from Stratford.

But Stratford and London are only part of the story. Recent years have seen a dramatic increase in the reach of the RSC, with major RSC productions on tour around the UK and abroad. Productions from Stratford and London visit regional theatres, while our annual regional tour continues to set up its own travelling auditorium in schools and community centres around the country. This ensures that the RSC's productions are available to the widest possible number of people geographically. An extensive programme of education work accompanies all this, creating the audiences of tomorrow by bringing the excitement and the power of theatre to young people all over the country. Between November 2000 and June 2001 the RSC will have presented over 40 weeks of theatre in more than 25 towns and cities in the UK, outside our own theatres.

In the past few years the company has taken Shakespeare to enthusiastic audiences in Europe, the USA, Australia and New Zealand, South America, Japan, India and Pakistan, Hong Kong, Turkey and Korea. The RSC is grateful to The British Council for its support of its overseas touring programme.

Despite enormous changes over the years, the company today continues to function very much as an ensemble of actors and actresses, whose artistic talents combine with those of the world's top directors and designers and the most highly skilled technical teams to give a distinctive and unmistakable approach to theatre.

THE ROYAL SHAKESPEARE COMPANY

RSC EDUCATION

The objective of the RSC Education Department is to enable as many people as possible from all walks of life to have easy access to the great works of Shakespeare, the Renaissance and the theatre.

To do this, we are building a team which supports the productions that the company presents onstage for the general public, special interest groups and for education establishments of all kinds.

We are also planning to develop our contribution as a significant learning resource in the fields of Shakespeare, the Renaissance, classical and modern theatre, theatre arts and the RSC. This resource is made available in many different ways, including workshops, teachers' programmes, summer courses, a menu of activities offered to group members of the audience, pre- and post-show events as part of the Events programme, open days, tours of the theatre, community activities, youth programmes and loans of parts of the RSC Collection for exhibitions.

We are building, for use worldwide, a new web site to be launched this year. This will make available all of the above, as well as providing access to the RSC's collection of historic theatre and Shakespearean material. It will also carry interesting and interactive material about the work of the RSC.

We can also use our knowledge of theatre techniques to help in other aspects of learning: classroom teaching techniques for subjects other than drama or English, including management and personnel issues.

Not all of these programmes are available all the time, and not all of them are yet in place. However, if you are interested in pursuing any of these options, or for information on general education activities, contact Education Administrator Sarah Keevill on 01789 403462, or e-mail her on sarah.keevill@rsc.org.uk.

JOIN THE RSC

For £8 a year you can become an RSC Associate Member. Benefits include:

* Advance Information and priority booking for our Stratford and London seasons (plus the RSC Residency if you live in the appropriate area).
* Special priority booking subscription scheme for the Stratford Summer Festival Season.
* Deferred payment facilities on Stratford tickets booked during the priority period (by instalments with a credit card).
* Special Members' performances for some Stratford and London productions.
* No fees payable on ticket re-sales in Stratford.
* Free RSC Magazine

Full members
For £24 all of the Associate benefits, plus:
* Guaranteed seats for RSC productions in the Royal Shakespeare Theatre, Swan Theatre and Barbican Theatre (for tickets booked during the priority period).
* An extra week of priority booking for Stratford and London seasons.
* 10% discount on purchases from RSC Shops.

Group and **Education** membership also available.

Overseas Members
The RSC tours regularly overseas. In recent years we've visited the USA, South America, Japan, India and Pakistan, as well as most parts of Europe. Wherever you are in the world, you can become an RSC Member. Overseas Membership is available from £15.

Special Overseas Members
All the benefits of a Full Member, plus:
* A complimentary programme for each Royal Shakespeare Theatre production.

For further information write to the Membership Office, Royal Shakespeare Theatre, Stratford-upon-Avon, CV37 6BB or telephone 01789 403440.

STAY IN TOUCH
For up-to-date news on the RSC, our productions and education work, visit the RSC's official web site: **www.rsc.org.uk**. Information on RSC performances is also available on Teletext.

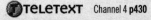 TELETEXT Channel 4 **p430**

A PARTNERSHIP WITH THE RSC

The RSC is immensely grateful for the valuable support of its corporate sponsors and individual and charitable donors. Between them these groups provide up to £6m a year for the RSC and support a range of initiatives such as actor training, education workshops and access to our performances for all members of society.

Among our corporate sponsors we are especially grateful to Allied Domecq, principal sponsor since 1994, for its far-sighted and long-standing relationship. Allied Domecq's announcement that its principal sponsorship will come to a natural end in 2001 provides an exciting opportunity for companies to form new corporate partnerships with the RSC, as principal sponsor, as a member of the RSC's new Business Partners programme or as a corporate member.

As an individual you may wish to support the work of the RSC through membership of the RSC Patrons. For as little as £21 per month you can join a cast drawn from our audience and the worlds of theatre, film, politics and business. Alternatively, the gift of a legacy to the RSC would enable the company to maintain and increase new artistic and educational work with children and adults through the Acting and Education Funds.

For information about corporate partnership with the RSC, please contact:
Liam Fisher-Jones
Director of Development
Barbican Theatre
London EC2Y 8BQ
Tel: 020 7382 7132
E-mail: liamfj@rsc.org.uk

For information about individual relationships with the RSC, please contact:
Graeme Williamson
Development Manager
Royal Shakespeare Theatre
Waterside, Stratford-upon-Avon CV37 6BB.
Tel: 01789 412661
E-mail: graemew@rsc.org.uk

You can visit our web site at **www.rsc.org.uk/development**

Luminosity was first performed by the Royal Shakespeare Company
in the Pit Theatre, London, on 20 March 2001.
The cast was as follows:

Susan Engel	Margaret Mercer
Karen Bryson	Debra Mercer
Simon Coates	Robert Mercer
Jude Akuwudike	Saul Mercer
Alison Newman	Betty Mercer/Midwife
John McEnery	Gardner
Timothy Kightley	Forbes
Ian Dunn	Skilton
Tom Smith	James Mercer
Niamh Linehan	Victoria Cotton
Daniel Cerqueira	Dalton

Directed by	**Gemma Bodinetz**
Designed by	**Kandis Cook**
Environment designed by	**David Fielding**
Lighting designed by	**Richard Beaton**
Music by	**Conor Linehan**
Movement by	**Melly Still**
Fights by	**Malcolm Ranson**
Sound by	**Steff Langley**
Assistant Director	**Emma Wolukau-Wanambwa**
Production Manager	**Patrick Frazer**
Costume Supervisor	**Jane Dickerson**
Dialect Coach	**Neil Swain**
Company voice work by	**Neil Swain**

Stage Manager	**Janet Gautrey**
Deputy Stage Manager	**Stephen Cressy**
Assistant Stage Manager	**Robin Longley**

Luminosity

Nick Stafford's plays include *Bad City* (Half Moon YPT, 1987), *ExtraOrdinary Behaviour* (Half Moon YPT, 1988), *Easy Prey* (Avon Touring, 1989), *The Canal Ghost* (Birmingham Repertory Theatre, 1990), *Back of the Bus* (New Perspectives Theatre Company, 1991), *Moll Cutpurse* (New Perspectives Theatre Company, 1992), *The Snow Queen* (Young Vic, 1992, and Manchester Library Theatre, 1993), *Listen with dA dA (Dreams Invadeth Man)* (Serpentine Gallery, 1993), *The Devil's Only Sleeping* (Cockpit, 1993), *The Go-Between* (Northampton Theatre Royal, 1995), *Grab the Dog* (Royal National Theatre Studio, 1995) *The Whisper of Angels' Wings* (Birmingham Repertory Theatre, 1997) and *Battle Royal* (Royal National Theatre, 1999). He has also written for radio and television and won the Dennis Potter Play of the Year Award in 1998.

NICK STAFFORD

Luminosity

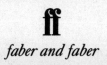

faber and faber

First published in 2001
by Faber and Faber Limited
3 Queen Square, London WC1N 3AU
Published in the United States by Faber and Faber Inc.
an affiliate of Farrar, Straus and Giroux LLC, New York

Typeset by Country Setting, Kingsdown, Kent CT14 8ES
Printed in England by Mackays of Chatham plc, Chatham, Kent

A CIP record for this book
is available from the British Library

ISBN 0-571-20988-2

2 4 6 8 10 9 7 5 3 1

Luminosity was first performed by the Royal Shakespeare Company in the Pit Theatre, London, on 20 March 2001. The cast was as follows:

Margaret Mercer Susan Engel
Debra Mercer Karen Bryson
Robert Mercer Simon Coates
Saul Mercer Jude Akuwudike
Betty Mercer/Midwife Alison Newman
Gardner John McEnery
Forbes Timothy Kightley
Skilton Ian Dunn
James Mercer Tom Smith
Victoria Cotton Niamh Linehan
Dalton Daniel Cerqueira

Directed by Gemma Bodinetz
Designed by Kandis Cook
Environment designed by David Fielding
Lighting designed by Richard Beaton
Music by Conor Linehan
Movement by Melly Still
Fights by Malcolm Ranson
Sound by Steff Langley

Characters

The Present

Margaret Mercer
Debra Mercer
Robert Mercer

1799

Saul Mercer
Betty Mercer (doubled with Midwife)
John Gardner (William Mercer)
Forbes
Dalton

1899

Skilton
James Mercer
Victoria Cotton
Midwife (doubled with Betty)

*Debra and Robert went to local schools,
so when they impersonate the Couchmans
the accent can be strongly regional*

LUMINOSITY

A walled physic garden in the English West Midlands, two centuries old. There are stone paths, the glimpse of glass in a greenhouse and the stone of a large house . . . Wood and earth and plants and trees and depth; a feeling of something behind and below; mass, denseness, texture. Earth and light. (And a large screen on which to project.)

SCENE ONE

The present. Margaret Mercer, a white woman in her middle age, tends the garden beds . . . a bird sings. Enter Debra, a black woman in her late twenties. Debra studies Margaret until a particular plant takes her attention. Her movement to it alerts Margaret to her presence.

Debra The woad's flowering.

Margaret Latin – without squinting at the label.

Debra *Isatis tinctoria.* Makes blue dye if fermented in stale urine.

Margaret Other colours?

Debra Madder to make red, indigo for blue, dyer's greenweed for yellow-green.

Margaret This?

Debra Clue?

Margaret Medical.

Debra Mandrake! I mean, *Mandragora officinarum* – Root used two thousand years ago to relieve agony of crucifixion. Mandrake gives Scopalamine, used today as a pre-med and a remedy for motion sickness. The myth of mandrake is that it screams when pulled from the earth.

Margaret Tree?

Debra *Quercus suber* – the cork tree. Hang a cork around the neck of a lactating woman and she'll dry up. *Cartharanthus roseus*; English?

Margaret Rosy periwinkle.

Debra Very good. From?

Margaret Madagascar, originally.

Debra Used in Jamaica as a cure for diabetes. How am I doing?

Margaret In what respect? What about this one? . . . No? . . . *Castanospernum australe*?

Debra Yes, yes, yes. Queensland chestnut, currently under chemical trial as an inhibitor of the HIV virus.

Margaret This?

Debra *Acocanthera oblongifolia* – a remedy against worms. And this, *Ochna serrulata*, used by Xhosas and Zulus and our family against stomach disorders. Do you know if William Mercer went to all those places and collected the plants himself?

Margaret No, I don't.

Debra The whole globe might have appeared to him a glorious seed catalogue . . . But.

Margaret But what?

Debra (*changing her mind*) It's lovely here. An oasis. A special place. And everything's so early.

Margaret Global warming.

Debra How am I doing now?

Margaret It won't be this easy.

Enter Robert, Margaret's white son, carrying a big box.

Robert Sorry, sorry, sorry, sorry. Late, late, late.

Margaret That's all right, Robert.

Robert Hello, Mum. Oh. Hello.

Debra Hello, Robert.

Robert (*beats*) I've got styrofoam rather than plastic (*cups*). Anyway, yes, styrofoam cups, easier to hold. They don't crack and make that irritating noise; though the children do seem unable to resist biting them. Orange squash. And the cakes. A magnificent array, as usual. Carrot cake from St Mary's Sunday School, ginger cake from the West Indian Ex-Servicemen's Women's Section; and banana cake from the Our Lady of Lourdes After-school Summer School Project. We have to keep track of what money goes to which place. Hello, Debra.

Debra Hello, Robert.

Robert Good to see you.

Debra It's good to see you.

Robert How's things? Are you famous, yet?

Debra Not really.

Exit Margaret.

Robert She's cross. I'm being too friendly to you. Ah, yes, she's cross. That's her cross walk.

Debra She told me that it won't be easy.

Robert Where have you been, may I ask?

Debra Thinking.

Robert Have you been thinking so hard you forgot how to use a telephone?

Debra Didn't my letters arrive?

Robert No letters, no, just cryptic messages.

Debra What's cryptic about 'I'm all right'?

13

Robert She's been down there twice, you know. She watched your flat until she saw you were physically okay.

Debra How's school?

Robert My infants are coming today.

Debra How's our property empire?

Robert It chugs along. Tenants arrive, we collect the rents, tenants mess up the properties, tenants leave, we refurbish the properties, tenants arrive and so on.

Debra You're cross, too.

Robert I've had to deal with her crossness. Just me. How's the life of an artist?

Debra Good.

Robert Getting work – if art is work? Is art work?

Debra I make pieces of work.

Robert Pieces of work? What are those recently: statues? paintings?

Debra Not necessarily.

Robert Then what?

Debra Pieces of work.

Robert Incomplete works?

Debra One work is a piece.

Robert A piece, not a whole?

Debra A section of a whole, perhaps.

Robert Not a whole whole?

Debra A piece.

They're playing, but deadpan.

Robert Is Professor Scrotum paying a visit?

Debra Why, yes. He might well be. And Doctor Knobhead?

Robert Hello, Professor Scrotum.

Debra Greetings, Doctor Knobhead.

The deadpan continues.

Robert I'm sorry, Professor Scrotum, I'm obviously not quite up to speed with modern art, but when someone asks me for a piece of cake this afternoon that's what they'll get; a piece of the cake, a section of the cake, not the whole cake.

Debra I said a piece of work, Doctor Knobhead, not a piece of a work. A piece made in a range of media: painted, sculpted; and I've recently been making three-dimensional structures from found objects.

Robert Three-dimensional structures?

Debra Made from found objects.

Robert Found, Scrotum?

Debra Things, Knobhead, objects, Knobhead, materials that evoke the subject.

Robert Then you stick, Scrotum, the objects together to make a piece about the subject?

Debra Stick, Knobhead, weld, Knobhead, cement, Knobhead, tie. Or sometimes I just throw them all up in the air and see how they land.

Robert You've been commissioned by the Tate? How marvellous! And can one tell what they are, these structures; can one see, Scrotum, that they are the subject?

Debra If you're inquiring whether sometimes the structures are abstract, then yes, Knobhead, they are.

I take whatever I find and fashion it into a piece which evokes in both its form and its content the nature and spirit of the subject.

Robert And what do you find? What materials?

Debra Whatever I source.

Robert Source?

Debra A piece is a work; to find is to source.

Robert Would that be tomato or hollandaise, this sauce?

Debra Ha ha, Knobhead.

Robert What exactly constitutes a found object?

Debra Exactly what it sounds like. An object I find.

Robert 'Finding' and 'sourcing' don't sound like the similes [**author:** ? synonyms] you suggest they are. 'Finding' something implies stumbling across it, whilst 'sourcing' implies actively seeking.

Debra You can 'find' something that you're looking for.

She smiles. He smiles. They remember how much they like each other.

How about you?

Robert I'm the one who stayed at home.

Enter Margaret.

Debra's moved on to making crap out of scrap.

Margaret I beg your pardon?

Robert Three-dimensional structures out of found objects.

Margaret I have no idea what you're talking about.

Debra He's teasing.

Robert She makes pieces of work and she works on pieces. Current project?

Debra I took an impression of my body in the classical pose of Britannia, then cast myself in white plaster, glazed it, added a dreadlocks wig, and draped the torso in a Union Jack.

Robert How does one take an impression of one's body?

Debra One removes all one's body hair, then one is wrapped in cloth impregnated with a resin which hardens. One wears a plastic shield over one's genitalia.

Margaret Shall we have a cup of tea?

SCENE TWO

1799. Enter Saul Mercer (black), and his wife, Betty (white). They settle and eat raw carrots. Off, children cry. Enter John Gardner.

John My master follows on behind.

Saul and Betty make pathetic attempts to clean themselves up.

John How are the carrots?

Saul Heavenly, thank you.

John Do the children enjoy theirs?

Betty Yes.

Enter Master Forbes (white), a Quaker. He's fascinated to see a black man for the first time.

John This is Mister Mercer and his wife.

Exit Betty to quiet the children.

Forbes When was thy last proper meal?

Saul Colchester, sir.

Forbes A hundred miles since?

Saul (*no self-pity*) We pawned the last of our clothes there, the last we could spare before we'd reveal us as the Lord made us.

>   *Enter Betty.*

Forbes And before Colchester?

Betty London, sir. Where we were married.

Forbes Are ye both from London?

Betty I was, yes, sir.

Saul I think I was born near Lake Chad, sir; north-west Africa.

Forbes Ye both speak well.

Saul *and* **Betty** Thank you, sir.

>   *Beat.*

Forbes Any diseases?

Betty No, sir.

>   *Beat.*

Forbes Here's a florin.

Saul *and* **Betty** Thank you, sir.

Forbes Can ye make mortar? This cottage is dilapidated; would ye pull it down and rebuild it?

Betty We can do everything.

Forbes Very good. (*He exits.*)

Saul Some carrots, a florin, and a job. Thank you, John.

SCENE THREE

1899. Kimberley, Southern Africa. The railway platform. Skilton (white) waits as a train disgorges its few passengers.

Skilton Mercer? James Mercer?

Enter James (white).

James Are you Skilton?

Skilton Welcome to Kimberley. Good trip?

James Long.

Skilton See anything of the Boer en route?

James A few horsemen, but no hostilities.

Skilton Is all this luggage yours?

James No, most of it belongs to –

Enter Victoria.

Victoria Hello.

James This is Miss Cotton. Miss Cotton – Mr Skilton, an associate of my family's firm.

Skilton I've only arranged accommodation for you, Mercer, I wasn't told to expect –

Victoria We met on the train.

James Yes, we only just met on the train. Miss Cotton's travelling to visit her family further to the north.

Victoria I'm only changing trains here.

Skilton This might be the last train in or out.

Victoria Perhaps I shall be lucky and there will be another.

Skilton I say –

James What?

Victoria Well, then. Thank you for keeping me entertained on the journey.

James I thought I was boring you, actually.

Victoria Goodbye. I hope it lives up to your expectations.

James Goodbye, then.

Skilton Goodbye, Miss Cotton.

Victoria Mr Skilton.

SCENE FOUR

1799. Saul and John companionably pull down the cottage.

Saul (*no self-pity*) I took the surname of Mercer after I was sold to a Dutch captain for two yards of check cloth, it being mercers who deal in cloth . . . The Dutchman sold me to an American in Barbados for fifty dollars, who in turn sold me to a minister in New York for fifty pounds. I was a profitable business. My price increased in every transaction without anything being added to my value. As to my first name, when I told the minister that I remembered my real name as Ukasaw, he said I should be called Saul, by way of the onomatopay, onomatopay, onopatopay, I can never say this word –

John What word is it?

Saul I know what it is, I know what the word is, and that it means a word that sounds like the thing it names. Otomapomay, onopato – I'm going to get it.

John I'd help you but I don't know this word.

Saul Onomatopoeia. That's it. Onomatopoeia, onopato-may – damn! Excuse me, forgive me. (*Deliberately drops brick on foot.*) Now I can swear – damn, damn, damn, damn, hell! Ah well, people have uttered worse and lived a long life. The minister made me a Christian and sent me to school, but when he died I was left penniless, so after a while I joined a privateer as cook, which is no place for a gentleman like you or me (*joke*), so I jumped ship in Havana and joined the Twenty-Eighth Foot –

John Our Twenty-Eighth Foot?

Saul You were in it?

John No, I mean, when I say our, I mean England's.

Saul We were fighting for England all right, I fought for England before I ever came here. Fought in Cuba and Martinique. Having fought for England, on my discharge I thought I'd come to England, expecting to find a Christian land. Oh deary me. I took lodgings in Portsmouth at a public house, the Beggar's Cat, and ventured out, leaving, in the safe-keeping of my landlady, my worldly wealth of nineteen guineas. When I asked for it back so's I could use some to buy a new suit of clothes, she denied I ever gave it her!

John Denied it?

During the following speech Forbes and another Quaker – Dalton (white) – creep to a vantage point to watch Saul. Dalton's never met a black person before.

Saul I argued and pleaded but she stood firm on her lie and I think I must have raised my voice, because a man dressed as an officer headed a crowd which pinned me against a wall – I don't now think he was a real officer – and it was demanded that I explain where I might have come by nineteen guineas in the first place. And I said it was pay from serving in the Twenty-Eighth Foot in Martinique and Cuba; whereupon this man who I do not think was a real officer informed the assembly that there 'weren't no niggers' in the Twenty-Eighth Foot; and the assembly, being made up of the inbred citizens of the locality, with low foreheads and crossed eyes, possessed of four fingers on one hand and six toes on the other – whose bodies, let alone their thoughts, had never travelled further than the next drain – believed him. And in a portrayal of pity which would rival any actress on any stage in any epoch, the landlady said she did not hold my false accusation against me, and that out of charity she would give me two guineas if I would be off.

John Didn't you want to kill that woman?

Saul As I walked away from that mob I imagined a tempest struck Portsmouth and hurled them out to sea, where they were lost. Then I met Betty in London, then came the children, then joy was our guest for a while, then destitution chased joy off. Joy – tears, tears – joy. Then here.

John I've never been anywhere. Nor my ancestors, neither.

Saul Let's have a look at your hands. Four fingers and a thumb on each. And your forehead is high, and your eyes both point forwards. Nearly.

Saul and John notice Forbes and Dalton.

Forbes John. Mister Mercer, this is Brother Dalton; my lawyer and friend.

Saul How do you do?

Dalton looks at Saul for an unnaturally long time.

Pleased to meet you.

Forbes After telling him about you, he was anxious to meet you.

Dalton Welcome to our country.

Saul Thank you very much.

Forbes How is thy work proceeding?

Saul Apace.

Forbes Good. Well, then . . . goodbye.

Saul Goodbye, sirs.

Exit Forbes and Dalton.

Saul What about you?

John Me? I'm one of the common herd, so I suppose, as I have no capital, my future will closely resemble my past.

Saul Ah, capital.

John With all the advances and inventions and new farms and factories and industries and trades and opportunities. With capital, a diligent man with a high forehead and eyes that point nearly forwards can improve himself. Mr Forbes has no heirs and no family, so as he looks favourably upon me I hold some expectations. I have given my all for him and I expect he will reward me.

Saul We've had no expectations. Only hope.

John You can't eat hope, but it can sustain you. Shall I tell you something absurd about me? Since an early age it's nagged at me that if only I'd been named William, my fate would have been different.

Saul roars with laughter. Enter Betty.

Betty Saul?

Saul What?

Betty The children.

SCENE FIVE

1899. A dop – a cup containing solder atop a tall copper stalk – holds the diamond.

Skilton Here she is. All two hundred and seventy-four and a half carats of her.

James Well, well. Well, well. (*He examines the uncut diamond.*) . . . No external blemishes . . .

Skilton None.

James Nor obvious internal flaws.

Skilton Believe me, I've looked.

James No sign of cleavage, fracture, or internal strain?

Skilton As far as I can tell.

James Matrix?

Skilton A Hottentot found it sitting in its alluvial deposits when the Vaal river was low. He took it to Farmer Van Niekerk as he'd heard there was a reward for such rocks. Oh yes, it was a hard bargain the Hottentot drove: two hundred sheep, ten heifers, one riding horse and saddle and bridle, one rifle.

James How much is all that worth here?

Skilton Up to five hundred pounds – depends on the quality of the goods.

James And we paid Van Niekerk £11,200 for it.

Skilton I bet Van Niekerk is out there now with the Boer horsemen. He'll be after the return of his rock if they take Kimberley.

James The temptation to dive in and attempt a cleave or

a cut is overwhelming. To see what lies inside, what facets, what scintillation, what colour, what light –

Skilton I'd put her away for now, if I was you.

James I better had. Thank you, Skilton.

Skilton How's home?

James England was dark when I left. What's life like, here?

Skilton It was improving all the time until the Boer's true nature emerged. We'd recently managed to lay out some golf links. There's an absolutely diabolical sand bunker on the third. Do you play?

James I'm afraid not.

Skilton You could learn.

James That is the most extraordinary raw diamond I've ever seen. I must sit on my hands.

Skilton Tell you what – sit on one hand, hold a scotch in the other.

SCENE SIX

1799. Saul's digging a grave.

Saul Then suddenly they complained of violent heat in the head. Then their eyes turned red and their breath became fetid, and their chests burned, and they coughed, wracking coughs tearing up their insides.

John Then the skin turns red, then come the pustules and the ulcers, and the urge to drink, and the urge to throw yourself in water, any water, and the rejection of any covering to the skin, for even the lightest touch is intolerable.

Saul You survived.

John But I don't know why or how. It's all over the village again. A cull. I'm fearless of it, now. It'd be a cruel God who allowed a man to catch it a second time. You must wear red, anything red, and eat horse manure, dry it and crush it and ingest it.

Enter Forbes. Completely swathed against pox.

Saul They have gone.

Forbes I am sorry. I am sorry.

Saul My children!? My wife!? Bury them. (*He lays the bodies in the grave.*) Are we sure they're dead?

He and John check thoroughly.

Let us pray.

They all do, silently.

And for John Gardner's wife and child who previously died of the smallpox. (*Beat.*) My family arrived in this place by accident and only lingered because we were offered kindness. God most certainly moves in mysterious ways. (*Beat.*) I cannot fill in the grave.

John begins to fill in the grave. Forbes coughs. Saul and John instinctively move away from him.

SCENE SEVEN

1899. A hotel lobby.

Victoria Hello, again.

James Hello?

Victoria I'm stranded.

James Stranded?

Victoria The line's been torn up at Styfontein.

James Really?

Victoria Really. Had to turn back.

James Is that it, then, are we under siege?

Victoria I don't know if it's quite that bad, yet.

   Beat. Eye contact. Swallowed smiles.

James Your family will be worried.

Victoria I shall just turn up there when I can. We've a very loose arrangement, really.

James You're staying here, in this hotel?

Victoria Yes. And you?

James Yes.

   Beat.

Victoria How long do sieges usually go on for?

James Until the besieged break out, or are relieved, or overrun.

Victoria Do the besieged ever surrender?

James Not on this occasion. Rumour has it that the Boer threatens to kill all the men and give all our women to the kaffirs. Oh gosh, did I really just repeat that to you? I'm so sorry.

Victoria It's all right. I'm used to such talk. In fact, I've heard worse than that.

James I didn't mean to alarm you.

Victoria I'm not alarmed.

James No?

Victoria Honestly, no. Have you seen the diamond you were so excited about?

James Yes.

Victoria Is it everything you hoped for?

James And more. I can't wait to begin fashioning it. She's in there, a beautiful, large, rare, cut diamond is in there waiting to be set free. Listen to me, off I go.

Victoria No –

James We diamond cutters can suffer terribly from nerves –

Victoria No, please, don't apologise. Your passion is infectious.

James Causing the crystal to split in an unforeseen manner, to become two, or three, or even four or more small gems is the stuff of our nightmares.

Victoria I can imagine, I mean, more than imagine, the way you describe it is so vivid –

James Would you like to see the diamond in its raw form?

Victoria Well, yes, I mean, I haven't ever seen an uncut diamond.

James Well you shall see this one, and if the siege continues for long enough then you shall see the finished gem. The before and after states, so to spea –

    Enter Skilton.

Skilton Oh, hello.

James As you can see, Skilton, Miss Cotton's journey has, as you suspected it might, been interrupted by the savage Boer.

Victoria Hello again, Mr Skilton.

Skilton I say, Miss Cotton, are you from Bloemfontein, by any chance?

Victoria Not from there, no.

Skilton Have you stayed there? I'm sure we've met before.

Victoria No, I don't think we have, unfortunately.

Skilton What about the Cape? –

Victoria I've never met you –

Skilton Is that where your people are from?

Victoria I'm sure I would have remembered meeting you, wherever it was.

Skilton My apologies. I didn't mean to be rude.

Victoria You weren't being rude. I shall wish you goodnight.

James But we shall fix an appointment.

Victoria I look forward to it. (*Exits*).

Skilton Feisty. You met on the train?

James (*mopping brow*) Yes.

Skilton You may have stumbled across a rare specimen for your private collection.

James For God's sake, Skilton –

Skilton Protest all you like, Mercer, you're hooked!

Margaret So. Your silence.

Debra I was thinking.

Margaret Was thinking; past tense. You've stopped thinking, now?

Debra I've been engrossed.

Margaret Did we do something?

Debra No, you didn't. No.

Margaret Have you met someone?

Debra Not in the way that you mean, no. I found this photograph of James Mercer.

The photo appears on the screen for our benefit. It's subtitled 'James Mercer with Pygmies in Kimberley, 1899'.

Margaret That's him, yes.

Debra Have you seen this photo before?

Margaret I must have.

Debra I found it in a book about Kimberley.

Margaret Oh, really?

Debra By accident. It made me want to start digging. I became – I am inquisitive about the family history. I knew the family had had dealings in South Africa, but I hadn't ever envisaged, I hadn't ever thought of any dealings between black people and that generation of Mercers.

Margaret It's not really dealings, is it? It's just a silly souvenir photo.

Debra Is it?

Margaret Well, as they aren't named, as they are labelled Pygmies, I expect it's the sort of thing everyone did. A tourist thing.

Debra I expect the Pygmies do have names.

Margaret Of course they must, but they're not recorded here. It's a Victorian thing; have your photo taken with 'the Elephant Man', or with 'the bearded lady'. Freak shows – and I'm not saying Pygmies are freaks, I'm saying that some people classified them as such . . . Does the book say much about our family?

Debra Not really. Not anything very insightful.

Margaret Perhaps you can you tell me the book's title – preferably before you disappear again.

Debra I wondered if there was anything you could tell me?

Margaret Are these trick questions, Debra?

Debra Do you mean do I already know the answer?

Margaret Yes.

Debra How can I already know what you haven't told me? Tell me about the Mercers and diamonds.

Margaret I only remember that when I was young our main business was indeed diamonds.

Debra Why did it stop being your main business?

Margaret I understand that grandfather James had a strong ethical reaction against Apartheid, and he instigated our own boycott long before any governments did, and we stuck to it, which is more than most governments did. Is that the right answer?

Debra And the family moved into property?

Margaret We bought up slums and refurbished them and let them to the poor. Apartheid overlapped with the fashion here for tower blocks, which I understand grandfather James thought were a disaster. So, serendipity; we were looking for new investments and people need affordable housing, proper housing. That's the version I was told. I was very young.

Debra What else do you remember about your grandfather James?

Margaret He was famous as a gem cutter, so I think perhaps that is why he was in Kimberley.

Debra Do you remember him as a person?

Margaret Yes.

Debra What was he like?

Margaret Lovely. Sad. Anxious. Hated bright sunlight – no, hated hot sunlight, wouldn't let us go out in it uncovered. Very wise, as it turns out, with all the terrible stories about skin cancers. Fed us *Ochna serrulata* every time we had a stomach ache.

Debra A tradition you continued.

Margaret It works.

Debra What was he sad and anxious about?

Margaret His wife Victoria, I suppose.

Debra What about her?

Margaret I never knew her. She died in Africa.

Debra What of?

Margaret I don't know.

Debra You've no idea?

Margaret There were more fatal diseases, then. And there was the war, of course.

Debra She died in the Boer War?

Margaret I don't think it was a direct result of the war, at least I never heard it was. I'm sure if she'd died as a result of the Boer War there would've been stories told about it. He didn't really talk about her at all, as far as I can gather, and nobody would have pressed him or pried in those days; reticence about oneself was much more normal. These days he'd've been on one of those terrible television programmes telling the world about how awful his life was. Victoria probably died in childbirth, it was very common, and he was too kind to communicate this to my father for fear of burdening him with unfair guilt.

Debra Is that all you know about James and Victoria?

Margaret I think so, yes.

Debra Have you never speculated?

Margaret No, not really. I've occasionally wondered, like most people do, I expect.

Debra How did people allude to them when you were young?

Margaret Allude to them? I can't remember.

Debra There's no real memories beyond what you've just told me?

Margaret No.

Debra Not even in your subconscious?

Margaret I suppose there might be something down there or back there or wherever the subconscious is.

Debra Something that explains you to yourself?

Margaret I haven't had much time for that sort of introspection. I still get up in the morning fully charged, and off I go until the batteries run out, generally at around suppertime.

Debra Do you know the maiden name of your grand-mother?

Margaret No, I only know her as Victoria. The story goes that her ashes were scattered here.

Debra Here in the garden?

Margaret Just over there.

Debra She's buried here?

Margaret Her ashes were, yes. In amongst the *Ochna serrulata*, rumour has it.

They look.

Debra So there is a story.

Margaret Yes, but that's the beginning, middle and end of it as far as I know.

Debra Do you know if she was English? I wonder if she was perhaps a Boer, and that might have contributed to his reticence.

Margaret I doubt he would have married a Boer at that time, given that the Boers were trying to kill him.

Debra These things happen.

Margaret He didn't hate the Boers, though. He'd tell us that if it weren't for the Boers, we wouldn't be here. And that includes you.

Debra Indeed it does. It's important to know your history.

Margaret It obviously has become so for you.

Debra That's partly because people ask me where I'm from.

Margaret Is that wrong?

Debra No, but sometimes, yes; no, not wrong – I mean, it depends who asks. When for instance another black person asks me, I know we have a shared understanding, but sometimes when certain white people ask it feels as if they're inquiring where – if push turns to shove – they could send me back to.

Margaret How tiresome.

Debra I think people should be forced to record their lives for their descendants.

Margaret We'd only lie.

Debra We wouldn't be allowed to lie, we'd be connected to a lie-detector.

Margaret That sounds rather draconian.

Debra Why did you adopt me?

Margaret Is this connected to your absence?

Debra Connected, but not the cause.

Margaret I know some people, especially some black people, think it's wrong that a black child is brought up by white parents, but given what's been shown to have been going on in children's homes, I think you'll agree that you and all the others were better off in a family, whatever the colour of the family – whether it be blue, green, or orange with pink spots –

Debra (*laughing*) Do you know any families of those colours?

Margaret You know what I mean.

Debra There aren't any blue or green people, are there?

Margaret Of course not.

Debra And if there were, they wouldn't carry the same charge as black and white.

Margaret Charge?

Debra As a child I prayed there were people those colours so it would become less significant that I was black.

Margaret I couldn't have any more children, we were well off, I wanted a daughter.

Debra A black daughter?

Margaret I thought you chose me, rather than the other way around. You pushed through the other children and held out your arms to me.

Debra It sounds like an incident at a dogs' home.

Margaret Dogs don't have arms to hold out.

Debra I do have big brown eyes, though.

Margaret And long eyelashes which you've always fluttered when you know you are being naughty. You answer me some questions, madam, like where have you been?

Debra In London.

Margaret Did my letters and calls reach you?

Debra I read all your letters yesterday. I opened them all as they arrived to make sure nothing terrible had happened, then I read them all properly yesterday.

Margaret I thought something terrible had happened to you.

Debra I let you know that I was all right.

Margaret But that is all you let me know. I've a dozen or so letters – well, letters is an exaggeration – a dozen or so pieces of paper on which is written 'I'm all right, love, Debra.'

Debra I had to do it.

Margaret Do what?

Debra Think. Dig. Consider. Exhume.

Margaret You wait until you have children of your own, then you'll understand what you've put me through.

Enter Robert.

And Robert.

Robert And Robert what?

Margaret I was trying to explain the effect Debra's unexplained absence had on you.

Robert I've told her that. I explained how I took all the flak.

Margaret Poor Robert.

Robert Poor mistreated Robert.

Margaret I haven't been able to marry him off yet, you know.

Debra Who'd have him?

Robert Plenty have tried, but I'm too much of a prize to give myself up easily. Are you ready for my infants?

Margaret Yes.

Robert Are you mentally and physically prepared?

Debra Have you ever seen this picture? (*James Mercer with Pygmies*)

Robert No. Is this what is known in the trade as a 'found object'?

Debra It might be.

Robert Are you making a piece about our family?

Debra I might.

Robert What will it be?

Debra I don't know, yet.

Robert Stand by to be 'sourced', Mother.

Margaret I beg your pardon?

Robert Don't stop still for a minute or Debra might consider you an object and 'find' you.

Debra He's taking the mickey out of art, again.

Margaret He's taking the mickey out of me; he's always doing it.

Debra I made a list of all the things she's done in this town.

Margaret That I've done?

Debra Please feel free to add things. Apart from the philanthropic housing you've maintained, there's also, in fact you've been chair of: Mother's Union, Meals on Wheels, St Mary's Hospice Fund-raising Committee, the City Art Gallery Steering Committee –

Robert The Design a New City Centre Square Competition.

Margaret The Design a New City Centre Square Competition Award Committee, actually.

Robert I do apologise, 'Competition Award Committee'.

Debra The Save Bignal Wood campaign.

Robert Was that a campaign committee, or just a campaign?

Margaret Just a campaign. And we won.

Debra The Say No to the Ring-Road campaign.

Robert The Raise a New Roof on the Cathedral Appeal.

Debra And you've been an elected Parochial Church Councillor –

Robert The first woman to be so elected –

Debra Local Councillor, City Councillor, Borough Councillor –

Robert Chair of several committees on each council –

Debra Why didn't you stand for Parliament?

Margaret I didn't have time.

SCENE NINE

1899. James shows the diamond to Victoria.

James There she is. She doesn't look much yet I know, but inside . . .

Victoria It was mined here in Kimberley?

James No, found washed downriver by a Native. A farmer gave him lots of sheep for it, so he's happy enough.

Victoria As long as he doesn't realise how much he could have got for it.

James He probably thought he'd put one over on the farmer. All those sheep for a bit of rock.

Victoria When did diamonds become so valuable?

James When we realised that a cut diamond of high carat is the most beautiful thing on earth.

Victoria What exactly is a carat?

James Originally it was the weight of a seed of the carob tree, but now it's been agreed at two hundred milligrams.

Victoria So, you cut one gem from this?

James Hopefully, one. I shall examine its crystallography – its internal structures – looking for any natural lines of axis. I shall shine light through it from all angles – various intensities of light, searching out flaws, looking for lustre – that is, reflected light; looking for intensity, looking for colour. Colour is an indication of flawed elements trapped within the crystal; for example, yellow indicates the presence of nitrogen; silver suggests aluminium, whilst blue-grey denotes boron. Colour diagnosis can be tricky because in some circumstances white light naturally disperses into its component colours, suggesting flaws where in fact there are none. Yes, terror strikes me but I shall assert myself. I shall procrastinate for some time. I shall lay siege to her, wondering where to make my first move, wondering if she will shatter if I approach her too forcefully or touch her in the wrong place, and before I take any sort of action I shall probably have an attack of nerves and be admitted to a sanatorium. (*Mops his brow.*) It is only when I have fashioned and polished the gem that I will truly know how pure it is.

Victoria This raw diamond is as complicated as a person.

James How so?

Victoria One can never tell precisely what is going on inside.

James Yes, one may be bitterly disappointed by what one uncovers, or elated.

Victoria The gem inside this is like its soul.

James Except there is no blackness within a diamond – only colours.

Victoria Black is a colour.

James No, it is the absence of light.

Victoria Oh? I shall remember that the next time I purchase a handbag, or gloves, or a coat. When I'm asked what colour I'd like the item in I'll reply, 'Absence of light, please.'

James Perhaps a white pearl is a better analogy of a human being.

Victoria How so?

James The pearl is a beautiful secretion that surrounds the grit.

Victoria The grit being what – fear?

James Very good.

Victoria Anyway, pearls are variegated in colour; they range from white to black – or should I say from white to 'absence of light'? Both are true analogies; the pearl appears beautiful but has grit for a heart, whilst the uncut diamond appears misshapen but has a brilliant soul.

Gunshots, off.

James An attack?

The gunshots continue but don't develop into a battle.

Victoria Someone breaking the curfew.

James Good grief, is it nine p.m.?

Victoria It's nearer ten p.m., actually.

James Is it? God, we're not exactly next door to the hotel.

The gunshots stop. Quiet except for dogs.

Victoria How much would it affect the value of the diamond if it had colours within it?

James Hard to predict. If a buyer falls in love with it, flaws and all, then they will pay what they have to to possess it. I've fallen in love with you.

Victoria And I with you.

James I really have.

Victoria Yes.

They're about to kiss. James collapses.

Victoria James? James? Can you hear me? James?

James only emits sounds of pain.

James, you're burning up. (*Searches.*) Where's the water kept? James, water. Over there? (*She looks.*) James, there isn't any. Does that mean we're out of water? James, you need water. James, I'm going to have to go out.

James Don't –

Victoria What?

James Leave –

Victoria What?

James Me.

Victoria I have to, for a while, unless you can stand . . .

He tries. He can't.

I'll return as quickly as possible, I promise.

James Might get shot . . . White flag, take . . .

Victoria James, you're not going to die.

James I . . . feel . . . terrible.

Victoria You're not going to die. Take this in your mouth (*the diamond*). Saliva, keep the saliva flowing. And for God's sake don't swallow it.

James almost laughs.

That's better. I'll be back soon.

James I'll die.

Victoria No, you won't. I promise you.

She kisses him. He's roused to try and kiss her back.

In 1799, enter John and Saul – who's preparing to move on.

In 1899, exit Victoria.

In 1799, enter Dalton, swathed against the pox.

Dalton I am executing Brother Forbes' will.

John is alert: Forbes dead?

In his last act of charity, Mister Forbes has bequeathed to thee this the land upon which you stand. Also what can only be considered a small fortune.

John Thank you.

Dalton Not to thee, to him. (*to Saul*) This draft is in thy favour.

Saul takes it and reads it . . . disbelief. He reads it again. He reads it again. He takes it and holds it so that if Betty were alive and she could see through earth she'd see the amount. Saul lets slip a mad guffaw.

John Excuse me, Mister Dalton, but I am, I mean, I was in the employ of Mister Forbes for several years.

Dalton He left thee three months' pay.

John is stunned by his meagre legacy, and Dalton lets him know that he shares his disbelief.

John Oh. Thank you, sir.

Exit Dalton.

Saul At last, I have capital.

John Oh? (*How much? How much?*)

Saul I am rich. And wretched. I could burn this, I am so numb.

He screws up the draft and casts it aside, but when John tries to retrieve it, Saul beats him to it.

John I should have made my life sound as hard as yours. Foolish, I was foolish. I should have followed your example, then I might have benefited as you have done.

Saul I did not ask for this.

John But somehow you appealed to his charitable instincts in a way that I did not.

Saul I wasn't aware that I made any sort of appeal.

John I gave you some carrots!

Saul Yes, and they were excellent carrots.

John And I brought you to Forbes!

Saul Yes.

John It is by my design that you have become rich!

Saul No –

John Yes!

Saul No –

*John tries to strike Saul but Saul stays his hand. A
struggle. John loses. Saul's disappointed as much as
anything else.*

*In 1899, enter Victoria. She inserts some leaves in
James' mouth.*

*James isn't watching Saul and John, but his torment
coincides with the next sequence as if a nightmare
looms up out of the depths of him.*

*John approaches Saul from behind, taking up a
brick.*

*An impulse overwhelms John; he raises the brick
and strikes Saul across the back of the head, then
staggers back in horror. He looks around for
witnesses, then watches, terrified, as Saul crawls,
dragging himself across the earth, reaching for the
sobbing John – reaching . . . reaching. Saul dies. John
finds the draft. He begins to dig Saul's grave.*

Interval (if there is one).

SCENE TEN

1899. Hotel lobby. James. Enter Skilton – armed and dusty and drunk.

Skilton Ah, Mercer.

James Hello, Skilton.

Skilton Have you started on her yet? On your gem?

James Still looking. Been out?

Skilton Just beating the bounds.

James See anything?

Skilton Took a couple of pot-shots.

James Have you been putting it away?

Skilton As water is rationed, one must avail oneself of whatever liquids are to hand. You've been working late.

James Yes, I have.

Skilton Is there a problem with the diamond?

James No.

Skilton I sense a feeling of unease in you.

James Normal nerves.

Skilton Have you seen anything more of Victoria Cotton?

James Is this leading somewhere?

Skilton You didn't make it back here the other night.

James No, the curfew caught me out.

Skilton All of us get caught out from time to time. The thing is, Mercer, you haven't been out here for very long. Old hands like us feel it's our duty to point out the lie of the land, especially the hidden hazards.

James Meaning?

Skilton Are you fond of her?

James I'm in danger of losing my patience –

Skilton She isn't one of us, you know.

James I'm sure we do not share the same perception of who is 'one of us', as you put it, because I do not consider you and me to be 'us'; and I'll thank you to mind your own –

Skilton A diamond may not show a single blemish, may appear perfect from the outside –

James Excuse me –

Skilton – but reveal its flaws when light is shone through it –

James What are these riddles?

Skilton I'm not being cruel, Mercer, but you've been taken in –

James Taken in?

Skilton Remember that I thought I knew Miss Cotton? Well I do, I did. Not me personally, but a chap like you, in Bloemfontein a couple of years ago. There's a bit of it about. You're not the first. Nothing to be ashamed of. It's a good act. The chap in Bloemfontein – a friend of a friend – formed a strong emotional attachment to a girl. He fell in love with her, actually. Lovely girl. Said her family were far away. After the attachment had been going on for a while, our chap sees her out one day, is going to greet her, obviously, but before he announces himself or she sees him, some feeling, a sort of premonition makes him stop. He says he thinks it was something about how the sunlight hit her. That's what I heard he said, anyhow. And he follows her, and she enters a strange part of town, not the kind of area he'd expect her to go or a place he'd usually enter himself, and –

James What are you saying?

Skilton I'm just telling you what happened. A story, a cautionary tale, if you like. There are certain things one does with certain kinds of women, but when one's considering falling in love, one should have regard for the family of the girl. Our chap in Bloemfontein, when he followed his girl –

James Are you saying this chap's girl was Miss Cotton?

Skilton I saw a photograph. Look, I've said enough, you've become agitated –

James What's the end of your story, Skilton?

Skilton My chap follows her to some house and discovers she's conned him. She has Native blood in her family, her mother's half-caste or something –

James punches Skilton, who falls.

James Get up! Get up, Skilton! Get up so I can knock you down again!

Skilton I'm going to overlook this. You've had a bad shock, so I'm going to let it go by.

James Get up.

Skilton I shall get up, but I warn you that if you attempt to strike me again, I shall take steps to defend myself. I'm only the messenger, Mercer.

James Just get out of my sight.

Skilton I'm sorry, Mercer, but it's better that you know now, before the attachment becomes too strong. We'll have a drink later, I'm sure.

SCENE ELEVEN

1799.

John Now the whole family.

John offers the draft. Dalton glances at it.

Saul Mercer said I should have it – he passed it on to me, it was his last request.

Dalton Thou hast that in writing?

John The end was sudden.

Dalton Any witnesses?

John's silence is worse than a verbal answer.

Did anyone witness Saul Mercer bequeath this draft to thee?

John No.

Dalton What dost thou want from me?

John I need a lawyer.

Dalton Why didst thou come to me?

John Because you were Mister Forbes' lawyer.

John's almost wilting under Dalton's scrutiny.

Dalton Half each.

John I keep the land.

Dalton The land where they're all buried?

John Half the cash.

Dalton If the draft can be cashed. I import iron ore from Maryland. It makes the best steel for the manufacture of gun springs, sword blades, musket barrels, shackles, chains and locks.

John Quaker guns?

Dalton John Gardner, isn't it?

John Can you cash the draft?

Dalton I can sell it, which isn't quite the same thing.

John William, my name's William.

Dalton (*gripping John's head*) I can see something terrible in thine eyes.

John struggles.

Let me look, let me look! Yes, yes. Darkness. Dark fires. Glinting horrors. And there, in that dark corner where the darkness is even darker, the extremities of a demonic beast? The beast is chained but it strains to escape the darkness. It snarls and strains to appear in the light. If it appears in the light you are lost! Keep it in the dark corner! Force it back – Har! Har! There, it is subdued. Now look into my eyes. Look!

John looks. John whimpers. Dalton lets go of John.

And that was just a glimpse. Thou shouldn't just change thy first name; thou shouldst become a Quaker. Quaker's are good. It's the master of disguises. Draw a Quaker veil over thy darkness. (*He gently undresses John and dresses him as a Quaker.*) Thee, thou, thy.

John Thee, thou, thy.

Dalton Thee, thou, thy.

John Thee, thou, thy. I shall become surnamed Mercer in honour of my friend and benefactor. William Mercer; that's who I am now.

Dalton Never let anyone close enough to look into thine eyes.

John Can you draw up my new papers?

Dalton Again?

John Canst thou draw up my new papers?

Dalton Bless thee, Brother Mercer.

SCENE TWELVE

1899. At the dop, James studies the diamond. Enter Victoria. He feigns to ignore her.

Victoria James?

James If only this rock could tell me its secrets.

Victoria That would ease your task.

James I'm beginning to wonder if this gem is what I thought it was.

Victoria Oh?

James It may not be as pure as I'd hoped. You asked if its value would be affected if it was found to contain impurities.

Victoria You said that was hard to predict.

James I was being too naive.

Victoria Perhaps you should rest from studying the diamond. You said it could drive you mad.

James The diamond tricks one into hoping. Stand here.

Victoria What for?

James What's the matter?

Victoria Nothing –

James Don't you trust me?

Victoria Of course I trust you.

James Then stand here. Amuse me.

She moves. He shines a work light on her.

Victoria James? You're frightening me.

James What were those leaves you fed me?

Victoria *Ochna serrulata.*

James That's the Latin name.

Victoria Yes.

James What's the Native name for it?

Victoria I don't know.

James You were in Bloemfontein, weren't you?

Victoria What's this about?

James Skilton did recognise you.

Victoria I'm sure I've never met him before.

James He doesn't claim to have met you, but he's seen a photograph of you, shown to him by a friend of the man in Bloemfontein who loved you. You tricked me!

Victoria Tricked you?

James I said I loved you after you'd tricked me into believing that you are something other than that which you are.

Victoria You took me as you found me, if my memory serves –

James Your trickery releases me from any obligation –

Victoria If you don't love me then you tricked me!

James Your surface appears white, but if one looks carefully you disperse into your component colours.

Victoria My family are respectable, did Skilton tell you that? My mother is a respectable lady and my father is a livestock merchant.

James And your mother is a half-caste.

Victoria I am not ashamed of that.

James Then why did you not tell me before –

Victoria Before what? Before when? Before you told me that you'd fallen in love with me? 'Dear Victoria, I have fallen in love with you.' 'Dear James, that's a pity because my grandmother's a nigger!?'

James Enough –

Victoria I fell in love with you, and you said, when I asked how colour in a diamond affected its value, you said that if a buyer fell in love with it they'd pay what they had to to possess it. You don't love me, then, because you will pay nothing. A love with no cost. If you'd rather you had the approval of men like Skilton than be loved by me, then your life will be as arid as the desert, and as unyielding as a rock, and if I go now, Skilton will have won. I saved you with those leaves. If my mother and my grandmother weren't who they are – if they hadn't taught me about those leaves, you would have died. I have no shame. The man in Bloemfontein, I knew deep down that he was insipid, but you, I thought you were . . . I am a gem containing beautiful colours . . . You said you loved me and you meant it. That truth will slowly kill you. No pearl will form around the grit that is your heart. (*Exits.*)

SCENE THIRTEEN

1799. John is checking figures. It's all very pleasing until he finds a perplexing entry. Enter Dalton.

Dalton A puzzle?

John This cargo on the ship *Perseverance* –

Dalton Yes?

John Four hundred pieces.

Dalton Yes.

John A 'piece' being –

Dalton A prime male Negro. Thou art comfortable with manufacturing and supplying chains, locks, branding-irons and guns – the tools and paraphernalia of slavery – but uncomfortable with trading in slaves themselves? I have built three houses for orphan children and I finance an apothecary for the poor. At Christmas Eve I have delivered a sack of firewood to every married couple over the age of sixty who reside within two miles of here. I could not afford these philanthropic acts on the twenty-five per cent return from trading in the tools and paraphernalia, only the one hundred per cent profit from trading in pieces allows me to benefit my community on such a scale. Name an industry in which we may engage conscience-free, an endeavour which does not involve some degree of misery for someone, somewhere, and will provide us with our present profits, and we shall throw ourselves into it.

John I shall endeavour to find one.

Dalton I would welcome that.

Beat.

John What is it, Brother?

Dalton I do not care to think what might ensue if any malicious person dug into thy past.

John Or yours –

Dalton Or thine!

John Or thine – what about thy past?

Dalton William, be quiet. I wish thee to succeed. I do not care about thy past if thou canst assure me that whatever thy secrets are, they shall remain buried secrets. Some Brothers, some very powerful Friends, have been voicing doubts about thee.

John Doubts?

Dalton They are jealous of our success, and if the rumours take hold –

John Rumours?

Dalton – it could be very trying, if not humiliating and mortifying. We have been called to appear before the Friends – not to answer to the suspicions about thee, per se –

John Suspicions?

Dalton – but to explain our involvement in arms manufacture, and our occasional interest in pieces. Thou shalt speak for us.

John I?

Dalton It shall give thee the opportunity to convince them that you are William Mercer, a Quaker brother.

I suggest you begin to prepare our defence – not our defence, our attack! Attack our attackers. (*Exits.*)

John (*paces . . . rehearses*) Dear Friends, regarding our investment in pieces . . . Dear Friends, do ye forget our philanthropy?

> *Saul Mercer, decomposing, shoots up from under John's feet and confronts him.*
> *John tries to avoid, then evade him, but Saul hounds him.*
> *A macabre and titanic dance/fight unfolds, during which Saul tries to make John look him in the eye, while John tries to push Saul back under the earth. John succeeds.*
> *John addresses the Friends:*

Dear Friends, to the accusation that gun-making is incompatible with our faith, I say that the manufacture of arms implies no approbation of –

> *Enter Debra, Margaret and Robert in the present. Debra is reading John's defence aloud. For a while both voices are heard and both times visible, then John and the world of 1799 give way to the present.*

John *and* **Debra** – offensive war, nor promotes war, nor increases its calamities. Moreover, I argue that it is unjust of you to single us out as all Quakers contribute to the purposes of war by payment of government taxes. If thou wouldst wish to be perfect, then refuse to pay government taxes and suffer the consequences. As to the accusation that slave-trading is incompatible with our faith, I say this: those of you who use the produce of the labour of slaves, as tobacco, rum, sugar, rice, indigo and cotton, are directly the promoters of the slave trade because the consumption of these articles is the very ground and cause of it. Abstain from consuming the aforementioned, then accuse us. Yea?

Margaret Where did you find this?

Debra In a library.

Margaret I didn't know about it. I've never heard of it before.

Debra You didn't know he was a slave trader?

Margaret No.

Robert It's in the small print of the family history, it's there between the lines, but I've never known it referred to directly.

Margaret Is this what you exhumed and considered and thought about in your absence?

Debra It's the main thing, I suppose.

Robert Can I be blunt? I know there's all sorts of ramifications, but history is history, it happened. Yes, one of our ancestors was a Quaker and invested in the slave trade, but what can we do about that?

Debra The ancestor, not one of our ancestors, the ancestor, the founder, the Mercer before whom there is no trace of this family. He made chains and locks and shackles and guns for the slave trade and he traded in slaves themselves. That's how he made our fortunes. I have materially benefited from that.

Margaret We all have; hundreds, if not thousands of people have benefited from the fortune William Mercer made.

Robert And everything we do now is guided by ethics.

Debra I'm not disputing that. But if we are ethical, what should we do, how should we respond to this knowledge?

Margaret I'm very sorry that our ancestors caused misery. I'm sorry that William Mercer financially profited from the trade in human misery, and I do sometimes think that I am sorry that our family went on to trade in the diamond industry in South Africa, but we've changed the whole way we think, we don't do anything like that now. We cannot be blamed for what happened before we were born.

Debra But the wrong has never been righted, there has been no redress, no reparation.

Robert Redress whom, Debra, redress whom?

Debra I don't know, you see, I don't know whom. But from my reading of our family's history, from my reading of how that fits into bigger history, nothing's ever been repaid.

Robert Repaid to whom?

Debra It was immoral earnings. He bought into an immoral system.

Robert But he didn't make the system –

Debra But he did exploit it.

Robert And his defence is more or less sound; he said, in effect, 'Let he who is without sin cast the first stone.'

Debra No, I think what he said was, 'We're all as bad as each other.'

Robert Which is the same thing.

Debra Slavery is definitely wrong, yes?

Robert Of course, I've already said –

Debra I mean, I don't know who my blood ancestors are, whether they're descended – whether I'm descended from slaves, but I do know that sure as hell if someone stuffed me, or if someone stuffed you in the bowels of a ship which disgorged us in a land where our language, our intellect, our souls even, were declared non-existent, we'd be –

Robert We'd all be, that goes without saying –

Debra So why wasn't it wrong, then?

Robert It was wrong then, but that was then. The contemporary conditions allowed it.

Debra Allowed it. Yes. But history, the shape of history, it's not a line towards . . . if history was a line on a graph, the line isn't an upward curve, it isn't a steady upward curve towards whatever, civilisation, perfection, whatever. No, it's a jagged line – there's things happened in Europe in living memory that make us look less . . . the Nazis fifty years ago weren't an upward advance, ethnic cleansing –

Robert The Nazis and ethnic cleansing we definitely can't be held responsible for –

Debra I'm not saying we are, I'm saying, what should we do, now? What should we say to each other? How should we be? I mean, we expect the Nazis to return what they stole from Jews –

Margaret For God's sake, Deb. Nazi this, Nazi that –

Robert Now, you see, now. What this is, this is political correctness. History is history. It happened. This revisionist stuff you're spouting is politically correct nonsense.

Debra You mean, 'Shut up, Debra.'

Robert No, I mean why try to change the past?

Debra Because the present doesn't make enough sense, because the present I know, that I live in, isn't explained by the past I have been told. Don't you dare accuse me of 'political correctness', don't you dare belittle or tell me to shut up or tell me to stop asking questions. You use 'political correctness' as a slur to stop debate.

Robert Is this a debate? I thought it was a telling-off.

Debra How can I tell you off, Robert? None of the sordid history of this family is anything to do with you, is it? It all happened before you were born. Look, I'm not talking about telling off, I'm talking about how our great-great-great-great-grandfather wasn't so great at all.

Margaret It's festering in you.

Debra No! It's questions, it's bubbling, not festering, it's not still, it moves, it's not rotting. I love you and Mum, I'm not trying to chastise you or gain any advantage from this, I want us to together talk about it, talk about it. Why did you adopt me?

Margaret You're asking me that again now?

Debra It's come up.

Margaret Then put it down.

Debra Why did you adopt a black child? The short answer, the potted answer.

Margaret You looked at me, I felt empathy, you reached for me.

Debra Remind me, how many children were there?

Margaret I don't know . . . Six? Seven?

Debra And how many were black?

Margaret What are you trying to read into this, what –

Debra Just me?

Margaret Just you were black, yes.

Robert We've got to stop this, we've got to stop this, this interrogation

Debra I love you, Mother.

Margaret I don't know if you do.

Debra I do. If I was to make a piece about you it would depict a good woman who tried to do her best by everyone who deserved it. You gave me a wonderful childhood and my life has mostly made sense until I came across the photo of James Mercer. Interesting. And I dig a little and I find William Mercer's defence. Disturbing, shocking. I make my piece depicting myself as Britannia. At the press viewing a critic appears in my face accusing me of 'political correctness'. He's livid. He's shockingly angry. He's almost puking with rage. His review is bile. Why, why, why? In the same edition of the same paper, there's a report that a black boy's been killed in a street by two white strangers who came looking for a black boy. Caught on CCTV, the executioners are arrested. Still reeling from the rancour of the art critic, I go to their court appearance and one of them glances up at me – a dark, chilling glance that I want to shy away from, but I make myself look. And he glances again and boof! Worlds and time and stories and history pass between us, a shared history, not black history or white history but our history, and two dark things, the look in this boy's eyes and William Mercer's defence, connect, and perversely, light shines. And it's clear that the reasons this white boy feels able to go out and seek and kill a black stranger aren't just the reasons he's found in his lifetime, it's decades of, centuries of, taut and sinewy and root-like memories, snaking under us, and I need to pull them up and untangle them and hold them up in the light and study them. And I'm not saying that it's only those white boys who need examining. Fucking hell! I'm fucking twisted inside. There's dark, twisted, tight fucking knots of anger and despair and grief in every fucking shred of me. Fucking, fucking, fucking aaaaaagghh! (*Beat.*) Broken stories; flickers of light, shards of truths.

Margaret Can I be honest with you?

Debra Yes.

Margaret Can I?

Debra It's your turn.

Margaret I think this business, this art business you've immersed yourself in is causing a lot of trouble.

Debra But?

Margaret I don't know. I don't . . . I don't know.

Debra Go on.

Margaret You asked something about the subconscious.

Debra I remember it came up, yes.

Margaret Well, I haven't been able to put it down. I made a joke about the position of the subconscious; below, behind.

Debra Yes.

Margaret I'm thinking about family, about history, about ancestors, about memory.

Debra Yes?

Margaret It's incomplete.

Debra Is it? What is?

Margaret I don't know.

Debra What's incomplete?

Margaret There's a gap.

Debra Yes?

Margaret A hole.

Debra A hole?

Margaret Not a hole, no. A something.

Debra I think I know what you mean.

Margaret Do you? Do you? Perhaps this is your territory; these are matters I find it impossible to articulate. There's an absence, but filled; a hole filled with shadows. It's position is back there, under here, but also all around . . . Now I feel silly, I feel exposed. I don't know.

The world changes. Debra has gone.

There's a broken line. Secrets. Whispered conversations. Swallowed confessions. I don't know. I can't find the words.

Margaret and, further off, Robert, stay on, sensing:

1899. Enter James, studies the diamond. Noises off: fireworks, cheers, music. Enter Skilton.

Skilton Brought you some champers. First train in, hundreds of bottles of the stuff.

James No, thank you.

Skilton I'll leave it here in case you change your mind . . . Thinking of having a go at her yet?

James I might.

Skilton Good luck. It's a good night to do it. You could call it the 'Relief of Kimberley'. Put more value on it, it being sort of commemorative and all that.

Enter Victoria.

Good evening, ma'am. Champagne?

Exit Skilton. James refuses to look at Victoria.

Victoria The trains are running . . . Are you going to say anything? . . . I'm leaving, then. (*Exits.*)

James addresses the diamond in earnest. He places a chisel on it, and strikes the chisel with a hammer. The uncut diamond shatters.

James Damn! . . . Damn! Damn! Damn! Damn! Damn! (*He roars.*)

Enter Victoria.

James The damn thing shattered.

Victoria turns to go.

Look, I do love you.

Victoria Can we leave here and start again?

James Please.

Exit both.

Enter John in 1799. He tells Saul's grave:

John The Atlantic Trade is to be abolished. Our new business is gems. I shall be good, from now on. I shall make reparations. In your name I shall be philanthropic. I shall finish and improve this cottage – no, build a house. A house! I shall start a family in our name, and have planted over you a physic garden. I shall make your graves an Eden.

Enter James in 1899. He paces. Off, Victoria screams as she gives birth. Silence. A baby cries. Enter Midwife. Blood.

Midwife Mr Mercer; I'm afraid I have to tell you that we could not save your wife.

James She died?

64

Midwife I'm sorry.

James She's dead?

Midwife I'm sorry.

James Victoria is dead?

Midwife She insisted we ensured the safe delivery of your son.

James Can I see her? Let me see her –

Midwife The nurse is preparing her –

James I want to see her now.

Midwife Let me look.

Exit. Enter with baby.

She would not like you to see her yet. Hold him.

He does.

We shall have to find him a wet-nurse. I know of a Native woman who should be pleased to help.

James A Native?

Midwife The milk is the same. Your wife saw him. She knows he is a boy. She saw him, briefly, and spoke to him, in Xhosa?

James I'm sorry?

Midwife She whispered words. It sounded like Xhosa. I'm sorry. My mistake. I'm sorry, it's just that one never gets used to these situations. (*Exits.*)

Enter Victoria.

James ?

James watches, horrified, as Victoria walks towards him. He almost cowers . . . She walks straight past,

65

in a parallel existence, and carries on until she arrives
at the ochna serrulata *in the garden in the present*
where she passes Margaret, who feels something but
cannot see her grandmother, who looks down, and –
for a moment – James, Victoria, Margaret, John and
Robert are in close proximity, then Victoria enters
the earth where eventually Margaret's gaze comes to
rest . . . Exit John, exit James another way. Margaret
feels a tug from both. Beat. Exit Margaret.

SCENE FOURTEEN

The present.

Debra I'm thinking of finding my birth family.

Robert That's what we thought you were doing in your absence.

Debra But I'm terrified.

Robert Of course, that's natural.

Debra What if I discover a history of something like cancer? Or they're poor and here's me, a rich girl who makes crap out of scrap.

Robert Or you simply don't like them?

Debra Or worse, what if I feel nothing for them?

Robert Your piece about our mother; I suggest a collage of photos of her superimposed over agendas of meetings.

Debra Silhouettes of her coming home at night, entering our bedrooms to kiss us.

Robert The first thing I remember believing about my father was that he'd died before I was born. Then I learnt that he hadn't actually died but was as good as dead because he'd left us. (*Starts playing.*) 'Is history a straight line?' Is it before? Behind? Or underneath? Or parallel? Or is it constantly at our elbow? Are we on top of it, like a ping-pong ball buoyant on a vertical jet of air?

Debra Good evening, Doctor Knobhead.

Robert Good evening, Scrotum. Professor Scrotum: is there, is it possible that there could be one history? One absolute, all-inclusive, truthful version? No, all versions are partial. A version is, by definition, partial.

Debra But my dear Knobhead, therefore all you are saying is that all versions of history are versions.

Robert No, I'm saying that all versions of history are partial.

Debra But we can adopt versions of history that more truthfully explain our present, Knobhead.

Robert Versions that partially explain our present, because all versions are partial, Scrotum.

Debra The versions of the past, Knobhead, the stories we choose to tell about our past, decide our present, and our future, Knobhead.

Robert I give up. You win. I know I'm just going to repeat 'all versions are partial' ad infinitum.

Debra You've never been able to maintain an abstract argument.

Robert That's because you hold some beliefs, whereas I hold none with any conviction.

Debra What do you teach your infants to believe?

Robert The National Curriculum says that they must learn to ask and answer questions. How to ask and inquire, that's the best I can teach them in the short time I have. You were asking of mother if she'd 'found' you or 'sourced' you, weren't you?

Debra Yes.

Robert You found each other.

Debra Yes.

Robert You sourced each other.

Debra Yes.

Robert Do you remember Barry Couchman?

Debra Me and Barry Couchman had a fight when I was twelve. He wore Cuban heels.

Robert He came up to me the first day you arrived at primary school. I was seven, you were five, he must've been six or seven. He said, 'How come your sister's a wog?' And I said, 'She's not a wog, she's adopted.'

Shock. Beat. They laugh.

I don't remember you fighting Barry Couchman.

Debra You weren't always there.

Robert Did you beat him?

Debra A moral victory. I'd just seen *Cool Hand Luke* on telly so I knew how to turn a physical defeat into a moral victory.

Robert You were a scary bitch.

Debra I still am.

Robert In the second year at comprehensive school I hit Barry Couchman with a desk.

Debra A desk? My big sissy brother hit someone with a desk?

Robert I was surprised, too. I'd been at comprehensive school a year, then you arrived. I'd had a year of respite from having to explain my black sister. In amongst a rising stream of provocative abuse, Barry Couchman included his opinion that you weren't adopted.

Debra Nothing that Barry Couchman said could surprise me.

Robert He said you weren't adopted, he said Mother had shagged a nigger.

Debra That says a lot about Barry Couchman.

Robert Doesn't it?

Debra That the most offensive thing he could . . . (*Tails off.*)

Robert What?

Debra Nothing.

Robert You were going to point out that the part I found offensive was not that he'd called you, in effect, by the N-word, but that he'd accused mother of having had sex with a black man. And that's what I did feel, then. I couldn't see the irony or the contradictions, just like when I'd said that you weren't a W-word but adopted. I'm not saying that's right, of course I'm not, but it's in me, it pervades my world. And I do think about it sometimes, but I refuse to feel terrible about it any more than I think I should feel terrible about my blood ancestors making a fortune from slavery.

Debra After my fight with Barry Couchman I realised that if I responded to every comment or act I'd end up in hospital or prison most of my life, so I developed an ability to imagine myself into the mind of someone who was giving me a hard time, and I'd see inside there an arid landscape, a mind with stunted horizons and dark skies, where nothing beautiful grew and no birds sang, and all was dull, and uninspired, and dying.

Robert You may not be festering, but you are bitter.

Debra No, I'm an artist, so it's my job to imagine. But yes, I am angry; why should I have to defend the colour of my skin – as if it needs to be or can be 'defended'?

Robert We evicted Barry Couchman's parents a couple of months ago. They were caught pushing their own excreta through the letterbox of an Asian neighbour.

Debra Was Barry involved?

Robert He's away, in the army.

Debra He didn't have to be like his parents.

Robert We probably do up to a certain age.

Debra Which age?

Robert Oh, I don't know. Something happens, we see things differently. It happened to you. It's not a fixed point.

Debra Their own excreta? What must it've been like in the Couchman household when Mr and Mrs decided to post their own pooh through their neighbour's door? 'What are you doing tonight, love?' 'What did you have in mind?' 'Well, there's nothing on the telly so I thought we might go next door and poke a turd through the letter-box.'

Robert I envy the man you choose. If he treats you bad, the superman who hit Barry Couchman with a desk will pay him a visit. You can see history here. Good history. However it was paid for, this is a physic garden. You can see on the trees where the side-branches were removed when – a hundred years ago? You can see time in the thickness of the wisteria, and feel it in the weight of the earth under the flagstones. Does your artist mind ever wonder why it is that the Garden of Eden didn't cover the whole earth? If Eden had covered the whole earth there wouldn't have been anywhere to be cast out into, would there?

Debra We should try and build something beautiful. A beautiful building, perhaps.

Robert What would it be for? What would be the beautiful activity housed within it?

He looks longingly at her. She glances at him, he looks away.
   Enter Margaret.

Margaret It's time for the children. Please don't go away again for so long.

Robert Hear, hear.

He opens the gate. We hear children's voices.

Hello, 2A.

A few voices answer, 'Hello, sir,' but most sound as if they're jostling and playing.

Line up, please . . . Bianca, did you hear me? Curtis? Curtis? Thank you, Curtis.

The children's clamour gradually rises.

Deepak, stop it. Yes, Deepak, you, that, stop that. Shanessa? Shanessa? Leave Bianca alone, Shanessa . . . No, Shanessa, it wasn't Miranda who pinched Bianca, I saw it was you. Simon, David, Jordan, Saleem and Shanessa, stop fighting! Cerise? Cerise? Shanessa! –

Sudden black and silence. End.